CHARLIE WAITE'S
VENICE

CHARLIE WAITE'S
VENICE

INTRODUCTION BY
JAN MORRIS

GEORGE
PHILIP

British Library Cataloguing in Publication Data

Waite, Charlie, *1949–*
Charlie Waite's Venice.
1. Italy. Venice. Description & travel
I. Title
914.5'31

ISBN 0-540-01190-8

Introduction © Jan Morris 1989
Photographs © Charlie Waite 1989
Captions © George Philip 1989

First published by George Philip Limited,
59 Grosvenor Street, London W1X 9DA

Design by Martin Richards
Printed in Italy

TITLE-PAGE ILLUSTRATION

A *sunset view of San Giorgio Maggiore, with
the campanile silhouetted prominently against
the sky.*

CONTENTS

To the memory of a dear and loyal friend,
Patrick St John Ives

and

*a Giuliano ed alla sua barca, senza il cui aiuto inestimabile
quest'opera non avrebbe mai potuto essere realizzata.*

ACKNOWLEDGEMENTS

I would like to thank Professore Alessandro Vaciago and Camela Treacher at the Italian Institute for their help and guidance, Dido Merwin for her constant encouragement, Jenny De Gex for her signposts and Lydia Greeves for giving me the opportunity to work in this glorious city.

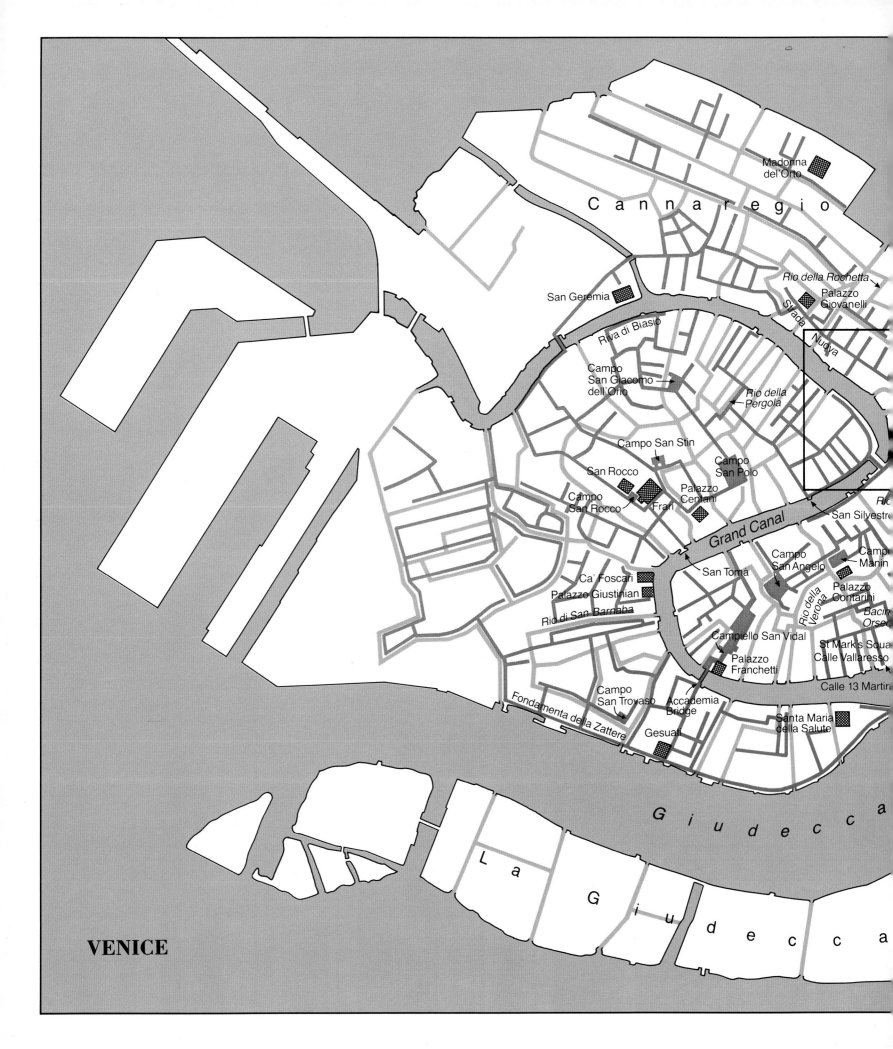

VENICE

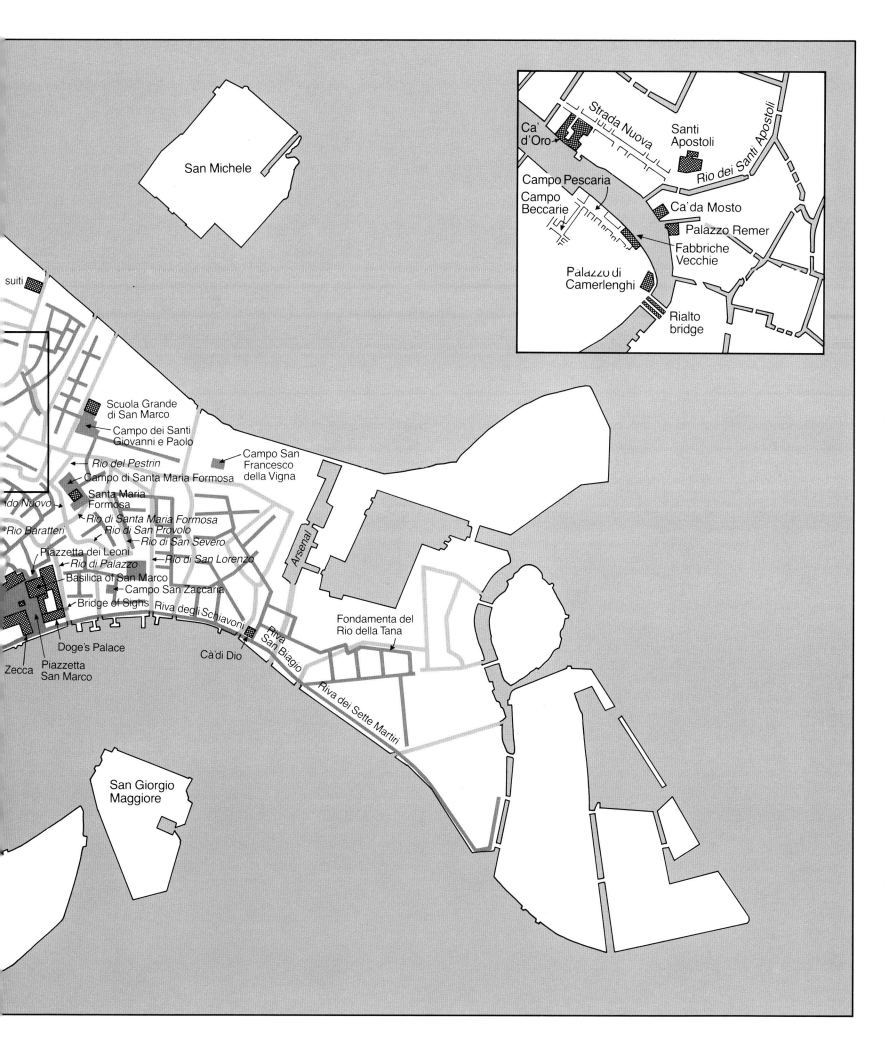

San Michele

Strada Nuova

Ca' d'Oro→

Santi Apostoli

Rio dei Santi Apostoli

Campo Pescaria

Campo Beccarie

Ca' da Mosto

Palazzo Remer

Fabbriche Vecchie

Palazzo di Camerlenghi

Rialto bridge

suiti

Scuola Grande di San Marco

Campo dei Santi Giovanni e Paolo

Campo San Francesco della Vigna

←Rio del Pestrin

Campo di Santa Maria Formosa

Santa Maria Formosa

ᵈo Nuovo→

←Rio di Santa Maria Formosa

←Rio di San Provolo

'Rio Baratteri

←Rio di San Severo

Piazzetta dei Leoni

←Rio di Palazzo

←Rio di San Lorenzo

Arsenal

Basilica of San Marco

Campo San Zaccaria

Bridge of Sighs

Riva degli Schiavoni

Fondamenta del Rio della Tana

Riva San Biagio

Doge's Palace

Zecca

Piazzetta San Marco

Cà di Dio

Riva dei Sette Martiri

San Giorgio Maggiore

INTRODUCTION BY JAN MORRIS

If, as Scott Fitzgerald once observed, France is a nation, England a people and America an idea, then Venice has always been above all an image. Peculiarly situated on a cluster of islands in an Adriatic lagoon, marvellously constructed, ennobled by great artists and addicted to prodigies of ceremony and display, the fascination of the place was essentially visual from the start. Those who saw the City-State for themselves were invariably amazed; those who knew of it only by hearsay evolved glorious mental visions of *La Serenissima*, The Most Serene, all glitter of gold, shine of marble, glow of onyx and ivory among its waters.

The Venetian Republic lasted for a millennium, and of course from time to time during its unexampled career other aspects of its character gripped the world's imagination. It could hardly be otherwise. Venice in its medieval heyday was the most formidable of maritime powers, and the mistress of an extended Empire. Its musicians and artists were pre-eminent, its craftsmen were unrivalled, its merchants and bankers made it the prime meeting-place of east and west. Its system of government, under the presidency of an elected Doge, excited mingled emotions of admiration, fear and sensationalism – if the stability of its institutions was the envy of other nations, its dreaded security organisations cast a chill across Europe. Until Napoleon put an end to it in 1797, the *Serenissima* seemed the one political constant of Europe, one of a kind and indestructible: as Voltaire injudiciously observed only three decades before the end, 'Venice has preserved her independence during eleven centuries, and I flatter myself will preserve it for ever'.

All these reputations were subsumed, though, as they have been ever since, in the stunning display of the place, which has impressed itself vividly upon millions who have never set eyes on it. 'I was never out of England', cries the man in Browning's poem, 'it's as if I saw it all', and there are many people in the world today who hardly feel the need to go to Venice, so familiar does it seem. It is this half-ethereal, apparently eternal, all but changeless presence of Venice that Charlie Waite has seized in the pages of this book.

First he has captured the city's essential homogeneity. Though its history is very long, and though its subject territories were once very wide, the bounds of Venice have been limited by its very nature. It was built upon mudbanks, protected from the open

Rio Ca' Bernardo off Campo San Polo.

Looking south across the Grand Canal from the Rialto bridge.

sea by a low line of islets, and only in the nineteenth century was it first connected with the mainland by a causeway. Down the centuries the small, tight sea-community that lived in the islands of its archipelago were accordingly able to make of it a unique stylistic whole. Many a deliberately created and planned city, like St Petersburg or Brasilia, has presented itself as an artistic *fait accompli*, but only in Venice, I think, has such an aesthetic unity been maintained through a thousand years of architectural change.

Few strangers, sailing for the first time along the Grand Canal which is the central highway of Venice, would be able to date the marvellous parade of buildings through which they pass. For myself, I would find it hard to guess at the age even of the Ca' d'Oro, perhaps the best-known of the Grand Canal palaces, which always seems to me, just as Charlie Waite has suggested it here, a kind of timeless and almost disembodied fantasy. Many of its neighbours strike me as equally uncategorisable, either because they appear to represent no particular period, or because they have been so enlarged, adapted, reconstructed, patched up or knocked about over the years that they can no longer claim to be of any specific time.

They range in fact from the thirteenth to the twentieth century, from the heavily-restored Byzantine warehouse called the Fondaco dei Turchi to the fire station erected in Anno XII of Mussolini's fascist era, or the white concrete railway station which went up in 1954. Yet with the exception, I have to say, of the railway station, side by side they constitute one of the most exquisitely harmonious of all urban thoroughfares, which twists with an easy elegance this way and that, below the enchanting bridge of the Rialto, past the mighty dome of the Salute, before it debouches estuary-like into the lagoon. The whole water-street, built over so many centuries, might have been devised by some genius architect all at a go.

In a wider sense too Venice seems to have established an arcane mastery over its own physical development. Much of its construction has actually been as piecemeal and opportunist as anywhere else's, and on the ground its canals and alleys can seem a maze of impenetrable confusion. Yet by some miracle all adds up to an almost ideal urban form, as functional as it is emblematic. Everything within it, the communities of the outer islands, the several quarters of the central city, the water-basin which is

OPPOSITE

The winged lion of St Mark, symbol of the city.

the harbour of Venice, the Grand Canal itself, looks towards the spectacular cluster of buildings, at the very core of the place, which were the original seat of Venetian power and purpose. Sociologically, technically, historically and symbolically the design makes perfect sense – Le Corbusier called it an object lesson for city planners – but most of all the effect is dramatically visual. The pink palace of the Doges, the exotic Basilica of San Marco, the adjoining Piazza which Napoleon called the finest drawing-room in Europe; these celebrated structures, presiding majestically over the island-studded lagoon, are like the focus of some tremendous canvas, in which the colours, shapes and allusions of the whole picture find their resolution.

Venice, in short, is a gracefully ordered whole. There are many individual buildings in the world so perfectly complete that one feels one could extract them lightly from their settings, as one might lift a model. Venice though is the only complete city that gives me this sensation – not simply because of its watery setting, but because every detail of it seems crafted to fit into the ensemble. A sense of organic balance, in which almost everything seems compatible, almost nothing superfluous or anachronistic, graces every district of the city, and makes all the pictures of this book, too, seem part of one grand composition.

Who could live in such a thing of beauty, without in some way defiling it? The Venetians themselves, the creators of this marvel, are only flesh and blood, and today they are supplemented each year by several million strangers from every corner of the world. This transient multitude threatens to overwhelm the character of the place, but its vulgar energy, noise, bustle and frequent philistinism are nothing new. Venice was made to be looked at, and from the very start people have come to stare. The Venetians lived like seabirds, marvelled one of their very first visitors, dispersed across the face of the waters, like the Cyclades! – and more or less the same sentiments cross the minds of contemporary travellers, 1300 years later, when they first see the towers and domes of the city rising from the desolate lagoon. The Piazza of St Mark's seemed perpetually full of Turks, Libyans, Parthians and other monsters of the sea, wrote a plaintive medieval observer – and that is much what fastidious moderns feel too, as they survey the tourist horde. Venice had Tourist Police in the thirteenth century, and one of the earliest of all municipal publicity slogans was devised by the medieval chronicler who suggested that the word *Venetia* really meant *Veni etiam* – 'which is to say, *come again and again*'.

There is no getting away from the fact that Venice is brazenly showy. It always has been. Byron called it 'a boast, a marvel and a show', and more than ever now it lives for its audiences. Wandering through it is like wandering through some stupendous stage set, a little too astonishing to be true, heightened, as though its perspectives have been adapted to fit the view from the auditorium, and its colours exaggerated for the footlights. Vast crowds down the ages have attended the great occasions of Venetian showmanship. In the old days there were the crownings of Doges, the victorious returns of admirals from distant wars, the fabulously ostentatious ceremonies by which the Venetians officially declared their Republic to be the Bride of the Adriatic. Today there is the newly-revived Carnival, a properly tumultuous successor to a celebration once notorious throughout Europe for licence and ostentation, besides regattas, art and cinema festivals, religious functions and the daily peregrination of the tourists through the city, preceded by guides brandishing flags, notice-boards or umbrellas like so many talismans – like it or not, one of the ritual spectacles of contemporary Europe.

Yet the presence of the city has survived it all. It has been menaced by the rising levels of the lagoon, by the subsidence of its foundations, by sometimes over-enthusiastic conservation, by the arrival of industry on the adjacent mainland, by pollution of air and water, by political and economic change, by war and foreign occupation, above all perhaps by the heartless corrosion of tourism, yet almost unbelievably it has retained its magic. It is as though Venice stands aloof to all that humanity can do to it, as though it has a calm and impervious life of its own, and realises that its image is itself – if the city were to sink to the bottom of the waters tonight, as I sometimes wish it would, the vision of it would remain for ever imperishable.

Charlie Waite has allegorised this sense of mystic permanence. Few people, few ships show in his portrait of Venice. The unforgettable shapes and patterns of the Venetian image, the towers and masks and bottles and gondolas, the mosaics of ancient floors, the façades of magnificent palaces, the well-heads, the wine-flasks and

A *window display for* Carnevale.

The enchanting watergate to Chiesa Zorzi in Rio di San Lorenzo.

market stalls, the ironwork railings, the marble staircases, the café tables — all are pictured here as though they have always been there, always will be, veiled in the light, it seems, of a perpetual early morning. This Venice would be as recognisable to people of the fifteenth century as it will be to people five centuries from now; and it is especially recognisable to me, for when I first went to Venice, at the very end of the Second World War, the city really was half-empty, a hush seemed to lie even on the Piazza itself, and in my memory time was suspended in a kind of twilight.

Of course there is to all noble works of art (and Venice is one of the noblest) a glimpse of the transcendent. Nowadays Venice offers us no ideological lessons. We do not go there as we might go to Washington or Moscow, Rome or Jerusalem, seeking grand evocations of faith or politics. Yet if we can ever catch the city in its stillness, as Charlie Waite has so often caught it here, it is resonant with messages. Nietsche said that when he thought of Venice he thought 'always and only of music'. Wordsworth called it 'the eldest child of liberty'. To Byron it was a fairy city of the heart, to Swinburne it was 'full of the mighty morning and the sun', Shelley likened its towers to obelisks of fire or sacrificial flames. Charles Dickens wrote a long essay in which the city figured only as an unexplained dream, and Mendelssohn translated it into some of the most lyrically joyous of all his melodies.

For myself, pagan that I am, I have seen Venice always as a God-given city, and the pictures in this volume only confirm the image.

1

THE GRAND CANAL

*Santa Maria della Salute,
Baldassare Longhena's baroque
masterpiece.*

The massive dome of Santa Maria della Salute dominates the eastern end of the Grand Canal.

Looking east along the Grand Canal from the Accademia bridge, the façade of Palazzo Franchetti on the left and the dome of Santa Maria della Salute in the distance.

The mid fifteenth-century gothic façades of the Palazzi Giustinian (where Wagner composed Tristan and Isolde *in the winter of 1858–9) and the Ca' Foscari dominate the right bank in the view east along the Grand Canal from San Tomà.*

The waterfront at San Silvestro.

A *line-up of gondolas at Fondamente del Vin, just east of the Rialto bridge.*

The Rialto bridge at dusk. Built 1588–92 by the appropriately named Antonio da Ponte, it was the only bridge over the Grand Canal until 1854.

RIGHT

Moonlight picks out the balustrade of the Rialto bridge.

The Grand Canal is at its most romantic in the evening, with a low sun colouring the water and catching the prows of the gondolas.

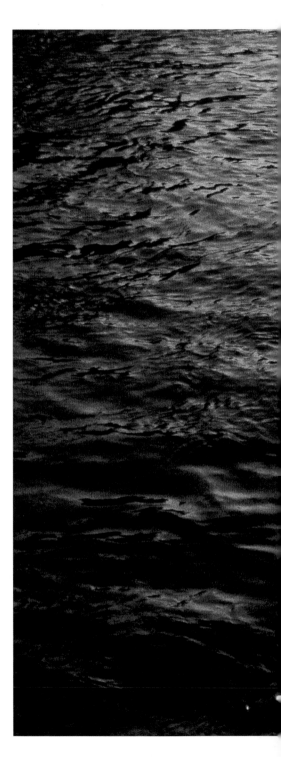

LEFT

Beyond the Rialto bridge the Grand Canal curves north-west, with Palazzo dei Camerlenghi, built 1525–8 by the Lombard architect Guglielmo di Grigi Bergamasco, on the corner.

A boat moored in front of the long, arcaded fruit and vegetable market, the Fabbriche Vecchie, with the campanile of Santi Apostoli peering over the façades on the opposite bank. The richly decorated thirteenth-century Veneto-Byzantine palace of the da Mosto family is second from left.

A *January mist obscures this view from the Campo Pescaria.*

The magnificent façade of the Ca'd'Oro, begun in 1424 and originally richly painted and gilded.

BELOW

Statues guard the water-gate of the palace adjoining the Ca'd'Oro.

The end of the day.

2

AROUND ST MARK'S SQUARE

Patterns of light and shade in the loggia on the first floor of the Doges' Palace.

Two of the five domes crowning the Basilica of San Marco. Founded in 832, this great church looks east to Constantinople, bringing a touch of the Orient to the centre of the city.

The Doges' Palace (right), with the domes and campanile of the Basilica of San Marco rising behind the façade of the old Zecca or mint on the other side of the Piazzetta. The Palace was the official residence of the dukes of Venice and the seat of the Venetian government from the ninth century until 1797, but the exterior of the present building dates largely from the fourteenth and early fifteenth centuries.

This porphyry sculpture on the south façade of San Marco is traditionally said to show two of the four Tetrarchs who ruled the Roman Empire in the late third century. It was carved in Egypt in the fourth century and brought to Venice from Constantinople at the time of the Fourth Crusade.

RIGHT

Doge Francesco Foscari kneeling before the Lion of St Mark above the Porta della Carta, the main entrance to the Doges' Palace.

Details of the carved capitals adorning the portico of the Doges' Palace. Some of these superb examples of medieval craftsmanship were replaced by copies in c. 1880.

Waiting for the tourist season: one of the cafés which spill across St Mark's Square.

The feet of one of the female figures guarding the entrance to the sixteenth-century Libreria Sansoviniana, the masterpiece of Jacopo Sansovino across the Piazzetta San Marco from the Doges' Palace.

Sansovino's marble Loggetta at the foot of the Campanile in St Mark's Square was crushed when the Campanile collapsed in 1902, but has been rebuilt using the original stones and sculptures. The bronze statues are also by Sansovino.

The balustrade of the Loggetta with the Doges' Palace beyond.

A *well-head in the Piazzetta dei Leoni beside the Basilica of San Marco forms a convenient perch for a photographer's model.*

A *drunken Noah on the south façade of the Doges' Palace leans away from the view down the Rio di Palazzo to the early seventeenth-century Bridge of Sighs. This covered way with its windows obscured by ornamentation is an evocative reminder of the prisoners who passed across here before sentencing in the palace.*

Giuseppe Soli's imposing neoclassical staircase in the Correr Museum at the west end of St Mark's Square.

Calle Vallaresso.

3

WESTERN VENICE

A *decorative well-head in a secluded courtyard off Calle Pestrin near Campo San Angelo.*

LEFT

Campo Manin. *A winged lion graces the monument to the patriot Daniele Manin who led an unsuccessful uprising against the Austro-Hungarian Empire in 1848.*

The late fifteenth-century spiral staircase – the Scala del Bovolo – in the Palazzo Contarini's open courtyard, which also contains a collection of Venetian well-heads.

One of the two late sixteenth-century bronze statuettes by Girolamo Campagna crowning stoups in the Franciscan Frari, a red-brick gothic church built over two centuries from 1330.

St Peter from Titian's Madonna di Ca' Pesaro in the Frari. The painting is one of two works by Titian in the church and was commissioned by Bishop Jacopo Pesaro in 1519 to commemorate a naval victory which he won against the Turks in 1502.

The eighteenth-century west façade
of San Rocco, only yards away from
the east end of the Frari.

RIGHT

The delightful courtyard of the
fifteenth-century Palazzo Centani,
where the playwright Carlo Goldoni
was born in 1707.

A *Venetian setting transforms even the most mundane chores, as in this scene in the Rio della Frescada.*

RIGHT

Rio de San Pantalon, just off Campo San Rocco.

In *Campo San Giacomo dell'Orio.*

Campiello *Squellini.*

*E*legant *Campo San Stin, with the*
characteristic well-head in the centre
of the square.

Rio della Madonnetta near Campo San Polo.

Campo San Geremia with one of the two well-heads in this square.

The Grand Canal façade of the mid eighteenth-century San Geremia from Riva di Biasio.

4

IN THE MARKETS

One of the colourful boats plying the
canals with fruit and vegetables for
sale.

In *the vegetable market.*

LEFT
A *detail on the arcaded* pescheria, *the graceful gothic fish market in*
Campo delle Beccarie.

Stocking up one of the stalls in the lively market in Campo di Santa Maria Formosa.

RIGHT

An enticing array in Salizada San Antonin.

Gulls wait their chance on the roof of the fish market.

LEFT AND RIGHT

In the fish market.

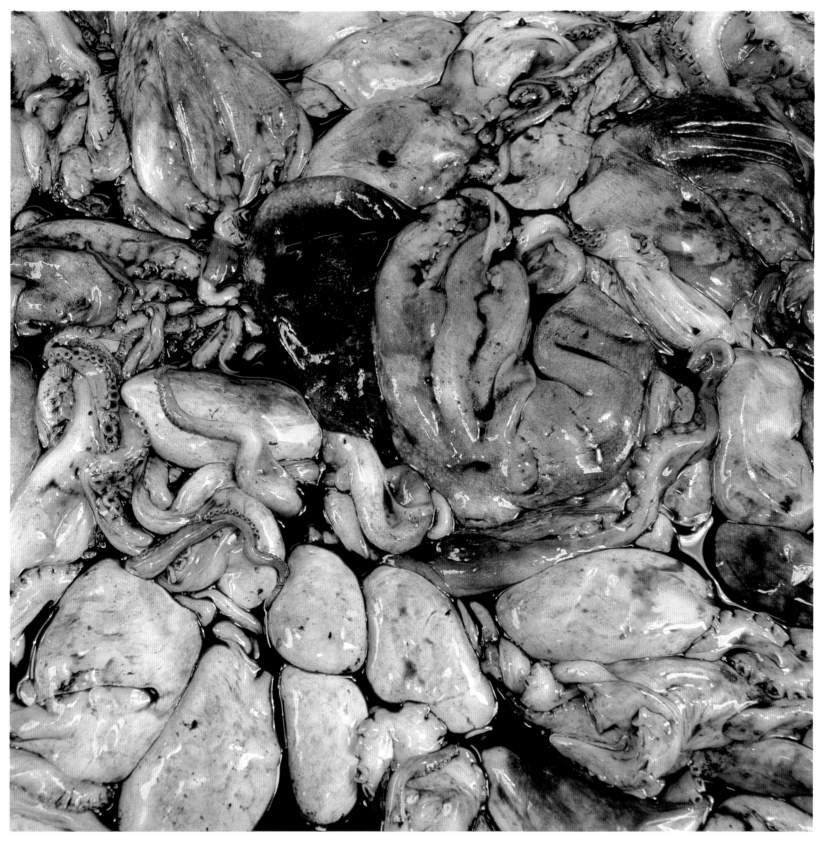

5

NORTHERN VENICE

The early seventeenth-century façade of Santa Maria Formosa, with its adjoining baroque campanile, looks over one of the most attractive squares in Venice, venue for a lively market; (top left) a detail from the church.

A *toy shop near Santa Maria Formosa.*

Rio del Mondo Nuovo.

LEFT

Rio dei Santi Apostoli.

The equestrian statue commemorating general Bartolomeo Colleoni (c. 1400–75) throws a long shadow in front of the sumptuous late fifteenth-century façade of the Scuola Grande di San Marco, with curious carved trompe l'oeil arcades by Tullio Lombardo either side of the main door. Now the civic hospital, the Scuola was built for one of the six great philanthropic confraternities of the Venetian Republic.

Palazzo Remer.

Two corners of the Palazzo Giovanelli off Strada Nuova and (right) *the delightful terracotta balustrade fronting the street.*

The lovely gothic façade of the Madonna del'Orto (left) fronts a quiet square in the northern region of Cannaregio. The statue of St Christopher over the main door (below) *is attributed to Bartolomeo Bon the elder.*

The façade of the eighteenth-century church of the Gesuiti, Santa Maria Assunta, is no preparation for the highly elaborate green and white marble interior.

6

CITY OF CATS

On the Riva degli Schiavoni: the winged lion of St Mark, symbol of the city, with a much smaller feline companion.

In *Campiello Piave: uncharacteristically, Venetian cats seem to enjoy each other's company.*

In *Calle de Forneri.*

Watching over *Rio detto Riello.*

Feline gymnastics.

In Campo Manin.

There are almost as many dogs as cats in Venice, perhaps descendants of the pampered beasts so often seen in Venetian art.

7

EASTERN VENICE

*In the Middle Ages merchant ships
from the Levant and Dalmatia
tied up at Venice's long
eastern waterfront.*

LEFT

In Campo San Zaccaria, a
quiet, leafy square dominated
by a remarkable part gothic,
part Renaissance church and
with house fronts incorporating
part of a former cloister.

Refreshment for thirsty
gondoliers in the Rio di San
Provolo.

In Campo San Francesco della Vigna (left), a stone's throw from the rio of the same name (above).

RIGHT

Riva dei Sette Martiri from across the lagoon, with one of the tall ships that must once have crowded the moorings here.

Fondamenta del Rio della Tana.

LEFT

One of the two colossal lions guarding the entrance to the Arsenal, a vast walled dockyard founded in the early twelfth century. The lions are spoils of war, brought here from Athens in the late seventeenth century.

Pavement cafés line the wide waterfront stretching east from St Mark's Square. The campanile of San Giorgio Maggiore is just visible over the balustrade of the bridge.

RIGHT

Looking towards San Giorgio Maggiore from Riva San Biagio.

8

BRIDGING THE CANALS

Sunlight catching the slender walkway over Rio Baratteri.

The spacious thoroughfare leading out of Campo Manin.

Multiple arches form studies in perspective over the Rio di Santa Formosa, the only canal in Venice where there are four bridges close together.

A flowing wrought-iron balustrade over Rio della Verona.

Ornate shadows decorate the steps of Ponte Borgolocco over Rio del Pestrin.

Enjoying a sunny spot by one of the bridges over Rio di San Severo.

Reflections complete the circle on Rio della Rocchetta.

9

CARNIVAL

LEFT AND OVERLEAF

The riotous Carnevale reaches a climax in the week before Lent, but it begins in January, when masked and costumed figures start to appear on the streets.

Mask shops such as these flourish all year round.

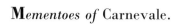

Mementoes *of* Carnevale.

Waiting for the party.

Some masks are humorous, some enigmatic, some frightening, some temporary creations of papier mâché, others stone figures which grin down on passers-by from arches and doorways.

LEFT AND OVERLEAF

Even the gayest costume assumes a sinister aspect when crowned by an impassive masked face and those revellers who dress predominantly in black seem to cast a chill on their surroundings.

10

SOUTH OF THE ACCADEMIA BRIDGE

Santa Maria della Salute *from the Accademia bridge, with the poles of Palazzo Franchetti in the foreground;* (below) *detail from a font in the church.*

A *water-gate just off Campiello San Vidal at the north end of the Accademia bridge.*

RIGHT

S*anta Maria della Salute, built as a thank-offering to the Virgin for the return of health (salute) after the devastating plague of 1630.*

F*ondamenta delle Zattere* (above and right), *which borders the Giudecca Canal.*

The *Dominican church of the Gesuati (below), built 1726–36 by Giorgio Massari, is adorned with statues and relief carvings (left) by G. M. Morleiter (c. 1699–1781), one of the best rococo sculptors in Venice.*

***C**ampo San Trovaso.*

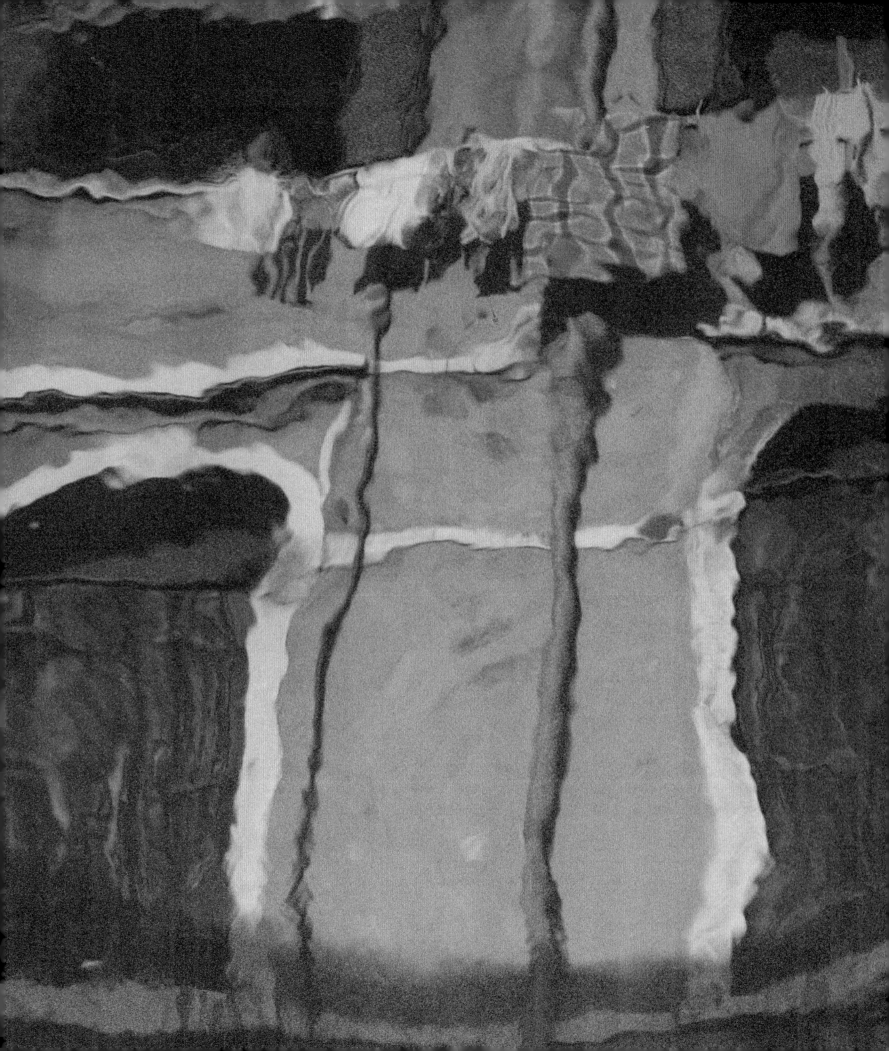

11

REFLECTIONS

LEFT AND OVERLEAF

Rio della Pergola.

RIGHT

Rio di San Barnaba.

Reflected sunlight dapples a painting in San Giacomo dell'Orio.

LEFT

In Bacino Orseole, behind St Mark's Square.

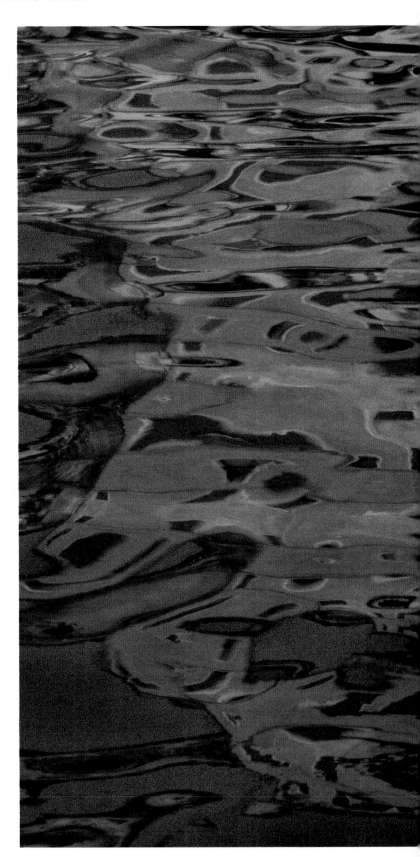

An ever-changing abstract painting on the Grand Canal.

12

THE LAGOON

San Giorgio Maggiore's temple-like white façade was designed by Andrea Palladio in 1565 and built 1607–10 after his death.

Seen from a distance, San Giorgio Maggiore seems to float on the water, its tall rocket-like campanile dwarfing the little lighthouse to one side.

The chequered pavement in San Giorgio Maggiore.

Calle del Forno on the island of La Giudecca, rarely visited by tourists.

The island of San Michele was laid out as Venice's cemetery in the early nineteenth century, when burials within the city were banned. (Above) Fog obscures the view towards Venice through the gates of the cemetery, framed on the other side (overleaf left) by a magnificent avenue of cypresses. The writer Baron Corvo (Frederick Rolfe), the composer Igor Stravinsky and the poet Ezra Pound are among the famous names buried here. (Overleaf right) A corner of the early Renaissance church of San Michele in Isola, set on the northern point of the island.

Beach huts flank the sandy beach of the Lido, part of the fashionable seaside resort first developed on this long, thin island about a hundred years ago.

LEFT AND BELOW

Glass has been made on Murano since 1292, when furnaces in Venice were banned because of the risk of fire.

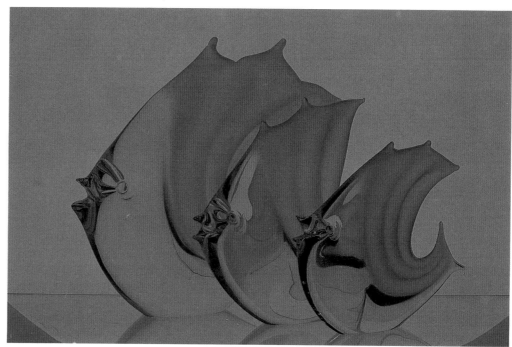

*F*ondamenta Daniele Manin flanks one of the waterways between the five islands on which Murano is built.

Waiting for collection on Murano.

A wall plaque on Murano commemorating the Russian ballet impresario Serge Diaghilev, one of the notable foreigners buried in the cemetery on the island of San Michele.

LEFT

A *tranquil corner of Torcello cathedral, founded in 639 but substantially rebuilt in the ninth and early eleventh centuries. This historic church is one of the few remains of the splendid town which flourished on this island until the growth of Venice and the ravages of malaria promoted a swift decline from the end of the fourteenth century.*

Burano *on an island north-east of Venice is a charming fishing village with cheerful, brightly-painted houses.*

In the lagoon near Murano.

INDEX